Where
Dinosaurs
Still Rule

By Debbie Tewell
with Gayle C. Shirley
Illustrations by David Mooney

FALCON PRESS®

Helena, Montana

Acknowledgments

The idea behind this book was that education is a key ingredient in resource protection. Duncan Rollo, who initiated the project, and Gayle Shirley, who went beyond usual editorial responsibilities, both solidly supported this belief. Harley J. Armstrong, curator of paleontology at the Museum of Western Colorado, and David M. Armstrong, director of the University of Colorado Museum, reviewed and commented on the manuscript in all stages of development and were advocates of the project from the onset. For generating enthusiasm for the book through his love of paleontology and his willingness to review text and illustrations, to answer questions, and to "talk dinos," sincere gratitude and recognition are extended to James I. Kirkland, a paleontologist with Dinamation International Society.

Copyright © 1993 by Falcon Press Publishing Co., Inc.
Billings and Helena, Montana.

Design, typesetting, and other prepress work by Falcon Press, Helena, Montana. Printed in Singapore.

Library of Congress Number 92-055078
ISBN 1-56044-177-1

Falcon Press distributes a wide variety of books and calendars, including children's books. You can get a free catalog by writing Falcon Press, P.O. Box 1718, Helena, MT 59624, or calling 1-800-582-2665. You can also get announcements of future books in the Interpreting the Great Outdoors series.

Contents

The World of the Dinosaurs

Long ago, in the misty past, dinosaurs were the kings of the earth. The time when they lived is called the Mesozoic (mez-uh-ZOH-ik) Era. It began about 225 million years ago and ended about 160 million years later.

The world was very different then. There were no humans. People wouldn't

walk the earth until sixty-five million years after the dinosaurs died out. At the beginning of the Mesozoic Era, all of the continents we know today were clumped together in one giant land mass. Scientists call it Pangaea (pan-JEE-uh). Gradually, this land mass broke up, and the pieces drifted apart. One of them became North America.

Scientists have divided the Mesozoic Era into three periods: the Triassic (try-ASS-ik), Jurassic (jur-ASS-ik), and Cretaceous (kre-TAY-shus). During each of these periods, the size and shape of the continents changed. The weather, the landscape, and the plants and animals changed. Even the kinds of dinosaurs changed as they adapted to their new environments.

About seventy-five million years ago—toward the end of the Cretaceous period—the central part of North America was covered by a shallow sea. The Rocky Mountains had only just begun to push up toward the sky. Volcanoes spewed ash over the West. In some places, the climate was warm and wet where deserts are today. When you stand on the plains of Montana or in the badlands of Utah, it's hard to imagine that some of this region was once a seacoast!

It's a little easier to imagine the unusual creatures who walked this coast, because their fossilized remains are still scattered across the West today. Hard-working scientists have unearthed many of these fossils and learned a great deal about the dinosaurs. Fortunately, they have shared their

Although dinosaurs such as these Acrocanthosauri *disappeared into the misty past sixty-five million years ago, you can see their fossilized bones, eggs, and tracks at many special places across the West.*

discoveries with the rest of us at museums, parks, and visitor centers—where dinosaurs still rule.

How Were Dinosaurs Discovered?

Humans have always been fascinated with fossils. Long ago, people found them, wondered about them, and wrote about them. Their stories were very different from the ones we believe today. Some people thought fossils grew from seeds in rocks. Others thought the fossilized bones were from giants or monsters that had been killed to make the earth safe for people.

Many years passed before the study of fossils revealed accurate information about dinosaurs. It wasn't until the early 1800s that people began to believe that huge reptiles once lived on earth.

In the 1820s, an English woman named Mary Ann Mantell was walking beside a country road when she spotted a shiny piece of rock. When she bent to look more closely, she saw that it contained fossil teeth. Her husband was a doctor who was very interested in fossils, so she gave the rock to him. She didn't know it, but she had made one of the first significant dinosaur discoveries.

Dr. Mantell saw similarities between the fossil teeth and the teeth of a lizard known as an iguana. So he named the strange, gigantic reptile *Iguanodon*, which is the Latin word for "iguana tooth."

It wasn't until 1841 that Richard Owen, an English scientist, concluded that the fossilized bones and teeth he was studying belonged to an entirely new group of animals. He named the new group *Dinosauria*, or "terrible lizards."

In 1877, two men made the first serious studies of dinosaurs in North America—mostly using fossils from Colorado and Wyoming. They were Othneil Charles Marsh and Edward Drinker Cope. The two men were rivals. They argued during much of their careers. Legend has it that their crews got into fistfights and even shot at each other! But by the end of their careers, Marsh had discovered eighty new species of dinosaurs, and Cope had found fifty-six. The two men are responsible for much of what is known about dinosaurs today.

Who Studies Dinosaurs?

The scientists who study dinosaurs are called paleontologists (pay-lee-un-TAWL-uh-jists). They study the past by looking at plants, animals, rocks, and other signs of life. They're able to find out interesting facts about dinosaurs by studying teeth, bones, tracks, and other fossilized remains.

To understand dinosaurs, paleontologists must be able to figure out how these animals were built, how their bodies worked, how they reproduced, and what they ate. They must also understand the dinosaurs' environment. And they must know about life in its present forms so they can compare it with what they learn about dinosaurs. In a way, paleontologists are like detectives looking for clues to a fascinating mystery.

Because paleontologists are still finding more clues about the world of the dinosaurs, information about these animals is always changing.

What Are Some Types of Dinosaur Fossils?

Fossils are rare. When animals die, they aren't usually fossilized. They normally decompose or are eaten. To become fossilized, an animal must be buried soon after its death, usually by fine sand, mud, or volcanic ash. Its remains must not be disturbed for many, many years.

Hard materials, such as bones, teeth, and eggshells, are most likely to be fossilized. But signs of dinosaurs can become fossils, too. Dinosaur tracks were first found in Connecticut in the early 1800s. The discoverer thought he'd found evidence of ancient three-toed birds. Since then, tracks have been found in many parts of the world.

Other signs the dinosaurs left behind provide clues to how they lived. Some dinosaurs swallowed stones to help them digest food. These rounded, shiny stones have been found with dinosaur skeletons. They're called gastroliths (GAS-troh-liths), or stomach rocks. Today, some birds swallow pebbles with their food to help digest it in the same way.

Coprolites (KOH-pro-lites), or fossilized dinosaur droppings, have also been found with dinosaur skeletons. They provide clues to dinosaur diets.

How Are Dinosaur Bones Dug from the Ground?

In the 1880s, fossil collectors hacked out bone and rock with picks, chisels, and hammers. Many fossils broke and had to be glued back together. They weren't always glued properly.

Cope developed a new way of collecting fossils. He wrapped the bones in thick paste before they were entirely freed from the rock. This way they would be less likely to break apart. Marsh improved on Cope's method and developed the technique that is still used today.

Modern collectors clean the surface of the fossil, photograph it, and mark its location on a map. Then they paint one side of the fossil with glue to protect and strengthen it. Next, they wrap it in wet paper and bandages that have been soaked in plaster of Paris. After the plaster hardens, they remove the rock from around the fossil, one side at a time.

A new technique uses aluminum foil and plastic foam instead of paper and plaster, but the steps are the same. Once the fragile fossils are in a laboratory, trained workers cut away the foam or plaster and clean the fossils. Then they tackle the puzzle of how to put bones together to make accurate skeletons.

Could Dinosaurs Have Been Warm-Blooded?

People used to believe that all dinosaurs were cold-blooded, or unable to keep their bodies warm without the help of the sun. Now, scientists think that most of them were warm-blooded, that they could convert food into energy and body warmth like people do.

One reason for this new theory has to do with the body shapes of dinosaurs. Skeletons show that dinosaur legs hung straight from the animals' shoulders and hips to the ground. This allowed them to move about easily, creating their own body heat. Lizards have legs that angle out and then down, so that their bodies stay low to the ground. They bask in the sun to stay warm. Because dinosaur legs were not shaped like lizard legs, scientists think they may have not have been cold-blooded. No one has yet proved that how an animal stands is related to whether it's warm- or cold-blooded. That's up to future paleontologists to figure out.

Some scientists also think dinosaurs were warm-blooded because of their bones. Living mammals and birds have many channels that carry blood vessels through their bones. Reptiles have very few channels. This could mean that warm-blooded animals have a lot of channels and cold-blooded ones don't. Dinosaurs had many channels in their bones. Scientists are still studying this idea.

A single meat-eater, or carnivore, must eat many plant-eaters, or herbivores, during its life. Fossils seem to indicate that in the age of dinosaurs, there were many more plant-eaters than meat-eaters. Because of this, some scientists believe dinosaurs must have been warm-blooded in order to maintain the balance between the amount of vegetation and the number of herbivores and carnivores.

How Did Dinosaurs Become Extinct?

For about 160 million years, dinosaurs dominated the land. Then, about sixty-five million years ago, they mysteriously disappeared from the face of the earth. Scientists have debated the reasons for this extinction ever since dinosaurs were first discovered. The only thing they agree about is that many species of plants and animals became extinct about the same time. No one has the whole answer—yet.

Some scientists believe the earth must have changed quickly in some way that affected all life. Some animals were able to adapt to the change and some weren't. Other scientists think many different changes occurred over a long period of time.

There is a thin layer of soft rock that covers the earth. It was created at the time the dinosaurs died out. This layer contains a rare element called iridium (ih-RID-ee-um). Below this layer, there are fossils of many kinds of plants and animals. Above it, there are fewer and fewer of these fossils. The iridium didn't cause the extinctions, but it's a marker that shows when dinosaur extinction happened.

Some scientists think the iridium came from a huge meteorite that hit the earth so hard it caused a gigantic cloud of dust. The dust blocked the sun for many months. Plants died because there was no light. Then the animals died because they had no food. As the dust settled, the iridium became part of a layer of dirt that eventually hardened into rock. Scientists say they've found a huge, buried crater in Mexico that may have been formed by such a meteorite.

In 1983, a volcano erupted in Hawaii. This gave scientists new ideas, because the volcano spewed iridium with its lava. As a result, some scientists have guessed that the ancient iridium could have come from deep inside the earth during an enormous volcanic eruption. If something like this happened on a gigantic scale, it could have caused extinctions, too.

Other scientists argue that acid rain or a gradual warming of the earth may have slowly caused the extinctions.

Since none of these ideas can be proved, paleontologists and other scientists are still looking for more clues. Whatever happened, the age of dinosaurs ended, leaving behind a vast amount of fossil evidence and a mystery to solve.

Seventy-five million years ago, a herd of centrosaurs struggled to cross a flooding river. Many drowned and were swept downriver, where their bodies piled up against the bank. Today, you can see their fossilized skeletons at Dinosaur Provincial Park in Alberta.

Where You Can See Dinosaurs

Some of the fossils the dinosaurs left behind are in museums today. Others have been partly uncovered and left on display in the quarries where they were found. And scientists still are searching for more fossil clues to the great dinosaur mystery.

Some of the places where paleontologists are still at work are open to the public. It can be a thrilling experience to watch the experts chip away rock from a giant leg bone that's millions of years old. Or to walk in the ancient footsteps of a fierce meat-eater hunting its prey!

If you'd like to stand on the very spot that dinosaurs once roamed, check out the following sites.

Dinosaur Provincial Park
Alberta, Canada

A herd of at least 300 migrating centrosaurs tramped steadily toward the river. The massive but peaceful animals approached their usual crossing point, but something had changed. Recent rains had caused the river to overflow and flood the cattail marsh along its banks.

Unaware of danger, the dinosaurs stepped into the river and began to cross. As the water got deeper, they swam, holding their heads high above the water. The younger and weaker centrosaurs had a hard time keeping up. They strained against the current but were too weak to swim against it. The rest of the herd went on without them.

As the animals reached the center of the river where the current was strongest, even the adults began to struggle. Some panicked and turned back toward shore. As they turned, they bumped into the ones still headed across the river. Soon, none of the tired, thrashing dinosaurs could fight the current. The swollen river swept them along. Many could not keep their heads above water and drowned. Dead dinosaurs tumbled over the living.

Finally, the river widened and the current slowed. The bodies of the dead piled up like rubble. When the flood waters receded, a heap of rotting dinosaurs remained. The smell of death attracted scavengers that tore the flesh and gnawed the bones. There was so much to eat that they left some bones untouched.

Over many years, other floods covered the bones with several layers of fine sediment that eventually turned to rock. The bones became fossilized. They were unearthed seventy-five million years later at the spectacular "bone bed" in Dinosaur Provincial Park. These fossils tell the story of the unfortunate centrosaurs, while other nearby discoveries indicate that they roamed in herds and may even have migrated.

Dinosaur Provincial Park is one of the richest sources of dinosaur remains in the world. It's located thirty miles (forty-eight kilometers) northeast of Brooks, Alberta. Seventy-five million years ago, this was a land of rivers, forests, and swamps on the western edge of a shallow sea. Today, it's a stark, dry landscape dotted with strange rock formations.

The park is the site of the Field Station of the Royal Tyrrell Museum of Palaeontology. Opened in 1987, the Field Station houses permanent and changing displays featuring some of the more than thirty-six kinds of dinosaurs found here. Educational programs, films, and guided tours are also available. And you may be able to watch scientists working on dinosaur bones in their laboratory.

Dinosaur Provincial Park has been named a World Heritage Site because it's

Careful excavation has revealed the spine and ribs of a duck-billed dinosaur at Dinosaur Provincial Park. PHOTO BY JOHN WALPER/ALBERTA TOURISM, PARKS & RECREATION.

fragile and special to the whole world. As a result, it will get the special protection it deserves.

You should allow at least two hours to see the Field Station and tour the badlands. Summer hours are 9 a.m. to 9 p.m. daily, and winter hours are 8:30 a.m. to 4:30 p.m. Mondays through Fridays. Admission is free, but donations are welcome.

For more information about Dinosaur Provincial Park, contact:

Chief Park Ranger
Dinosaur Provincial Park
Box 60
Patricia, Alberta
CANADA T0J 2K0
(403) 378-4342

Petrified Forest National Park
Arizona

The stream wandered slowly through the forest before emptying into a still pond. The air was humid and smelled of rotting plants. Light filtered through the trees, dappling the pond's surface. Leaves floated on the water, and fallen trees littered the banks.

The jumble of logs made a perfect hiding place for a small group of phytosaurs. They looked like crocodiles, with their scaly skin, short legs, long, narrow snouts, and sharp teeth. They waited patiently to grab and eat any animal that might come to the pond to drink, or any swimming animal that might venture too far onto shore.

A graceful *Coelophysis* darted toward the water but disappeared into a thicket when it spotted the phytosaurs. A large phytosaur snapped at the retreating dinosaur. It missed and snagged the thorny skin of one of its own kind instead. The injured phytosaur wheeled around and bit its attacker on the snout. Furious, the two lumbering animals fought, rolling over each other until they fell into the water. The splash broke the silence of the forest and alerted the other animals to danger. A *Metoposaurus*, a large meat-eating amphibian that lived in the water, glided quickly away from the tangling phytosaurs.

When the two animals separated, they returned to the cover of the fallen trees. They hadn't injured each other seriously, but their wounds hurt and could easily become infected.

This little drama may well have unfolded 225 million years ago in the area

A model of Coelophysis, *one of the earliest dinosaurs, is on display at Petrified Forest National Park.* PHOTO BY TERRY MAZE/NATIONAL PARK SERVICE.

that is now Petrified Forest National Park. Fossils of phytosaurs, *Coelophysis*, and *Metoposaurus* have been found in the park. They are remarkable because these three creatures lived very early in the age of dinosaurs.

Phytosaurs were not dinosaurs. They were ancient reptiles on the verge of becoming extinct as the first dinosaurs walked the earth. *Coelophysis*, a small, birdlike meat-eater, was one of the earliest dinosaurs.

Petrified Forest National Park was first set aside in 1906 to protect the large, fossilized trees found here. But many other relics of ancient times have been discovered here, too. More than 200 plants and sixty animals have been identified from remains found at Petrified Forest. The fossils date from the time of the earliest known dinosaurs.

Petrified Forest National Park is 115 miles east of Flagstaff, Arizona, on Interstate 40. Admission is $5 per vehicle. Days and hours of operation vary throughout the year, so call or write the park before you visit.

Petrified Forest National Park
Box 2217
Petrified Forest, Arizona 86028
(602) 524-6228

A graceful Coelophysis flees the snapping jaws of some crocodile-like phytosaurs. The fossilized remains of both creatures are on display at Petrified Forest National Park in Arizona. They're remarkable because they're 225 million years old.

Dinosaur Ridge
Colorado

A broad, flat expanse of seashore stretched far into the distance. Low hills squatted on the horizon. Small groups of *Iguanodon*-like dinosaurs fed on leaves from the lower branches of the trees that dotted the shoreline. Others wandered in and out of the trees, some alone and others in groups. None seemed to be in a hurry.

Three dinosaurs walked side by side, following the shoreline. Their large hind feet sank more deeply into the mud than their smaller front feet. It was easy to walk long distances on the mud because it had been packed hard by the sea. For just this reason, many dinosaurs used the shoreline to travel from place to place. Millions of their tracks marred the coast.

Uncovered 100 million years later at Dinosaur Ridge, the fossilized tracks of these three dinosaurs tell a story. It isn't a dramatic story of hunter and prey. But it's a story that gives paleontologists an insight into dinosaur life.

Long ago, scientists thought that *Iguanodon*-like dinosaurs walked on their hind legs, holding their short front legs against their chests. These tracks distinctly show the impressions of both hind and front feet. As a result, scientists now know that these dinosaurs sometimes walked on all four feet.

The other interesting thing about the tracks at Dinosaur Ridge is that they show that plant-eating dinosaurs traveled in groups. Tracks in other places indicate the same thing.

Heavily traveled shorelines like this one have been called "dinosaur freeways." Some experts think the freeways might have been migration routes. But no one knows for certain yet whether dinosaurs moved from one place to another when the seasons changed.

Dinosaur Ridge has been the site of important dinosaur research and fossil collection since the late 1800s, when O.C. Marsh first discovered the bones of *Stegosaurus* and *Apatosaurus* here. Today, there is a mile-long, self-guided automobile trail with fifteen stops where you can learn about dinosaurs and local geology and ecology.

The Morrison Natural History Museum near Denver serves as an information center for people interested in Dinosaur Ridge. You can get a free brochure or buy a thirty-page booklet on Dinosaur Ridge at the museum.

You can get to the Morrison Natural History Museum by taking Interstate 70 west from Denver to Highway 26. Drive south for three miles on Highway 26 to the town of Morrison. Turn west onto Highway 74 in Morrison and go a quarter of a mile to Highway 8. Go half a mile south on Highway 8. Call ahead to find out when the museum is open.

You can get to Dinosaur Ridge by taking Interstate 70 west from Denver to Highway 26. Head south on Highway 26 and follow the signs onto the ridge on the east side of the road. Numbered posts show where to stop for information.

Morrison Natural History Museum/Dinosaur Ridge
P.O. Box 564
Morrison, Colorado 80465
(303) 697-1873

Dinosaur Ridge, Colorado, was once a "dinosaur freeway" traveled by several kinds of dinosaurs, including the Iguanodon *whose footprint is shown here.* PHOTOS COURTESY OF FRIENDS OF DINOSAUR RIDGE.

One hundred million years have passed since these Iguanodon-*like dinosaurs walked the shoreline of an inland sea. Their fossilized footprints, or tracks, are one of the main attractions at Dinosaur Ridge in Colorado.*

Rabbit Valley
Colorado

The land was flat and dry except for a single watering hole, where dinosaurs gathered to drink. Trees and plants crowded against the water. Fish swam beneath its surface, and snails crawled along its banks.

The watering hole bustled with activity. Plant-eaters approached it warily, on guard against predators. Meat-eaters, knowing their prey would have to drink, hid silently in clumps of nearby plants. The air was thick with danger. Everyday, careless dinosaurs were attacked and killed here. Their bones littered the bottom and banks of the pond.

Miles away, in what is now Nevada, volcanoes sometimes erupted. Gradually, their ash dusted the land and sank to the bottom of the pond, covering the dead dinosaurs. Eventually, the dinosaur remains—bones, teeth, spines, and armor—became fossilized.

The story paleontologists can read at Rabbit Valley is a fascinating one. Fossilized ferns, pollen, and conifer logs tell of the rich variety of plants that surrounded the dinosaurs who lived in what is now western Colorado.

Scientists found an *Apatosaurus* here that may be the largest ever discovered. One of its vertebrae is six feet wide and five feet high! Paleontologists are now working to unearth the huge skull that sat atop the neck.

Many kinds of dinosaurs must have used the ancient watering hole. Scientists have found the remains of *Diplodocus, Camarasaurus, Ceratosaurus, Allosaurus*, and possibly *Brachiosaurus*. They found the scattered side spikes and armor of a nodosaur that was probably eaten by another dinosaur. This is the first nodosaur ever found in this particular layer of rock. The species must have lived much earlier in North America than paleontologists once thought.

One creature that was close to extinction when it was fossilized at Rabbit Valley was a fish whose Latin name is *Coccolepsis robelaisi*. Similar remains have always been found in older rock. The fish had never before been found in the company of dinosaurs. Paleontologists know that it was a very uncommon animal during this time period.

Rabbit Valley Research Natural Area is operated by the Bureau of Land Management and the Museum of Western Colorado. You can hike through the valley on a self-guided trail known as the "Trail Through Time." Along the way, you'll see parts of the skeletons of *Camarasaurus* and *Diplodocus* still sticking out of the rock. You'll also see evidence of ancient floods and the fossils of dinosaur bones that were broken as they rolled down an ancient stream.

To get to Rabbit Valley, travel thirty miles west of Grand Junction, Colorado, on Interstate 70 to the Rabbit Valley exit. Park north of the off ramp. The self-guided trail begins at the parking lot.

Dinamation International Society offers Dinosaur Discovery Expeditions to several dig sites, including Rabbit Valley. Participants have made some exciting fossil discoveries. To find out more about the expeditions, contact:

> Dinamation International Society
> P.O. Box 307
> Fruita, Colorado 81521
> 1-800-547-0503 (toll-free)

For more information about Rabbit Valley, contact:

> Museum of Western Colorado
> P.O. Box 20,000-5020
> Grand Junction, Colorado 81502-5020
> (303) 242-0971

Left. *Six half-sized robotic dinosaurs, including the* Corythosaurus *at left, are popular attractions at the Museum of Western Colorado's Dinosaur Valley Exhibit in Grand Junction.* PHOTO BY AL LIGRANI/MUSEUM OF WESTERN COLORADO.

Right. *A student at the museum examines dinosaur eggshell fragments through a microscope.* PHOTO BY JANICE LYNN SUNSHINE/MUSEUM OF WESTERN COLORADO.

The drama of the hunter and the hunted was played out often at this watering hole, which existed millions of years ago in what is now western Colorado. The remains of the meat-eater Ceratosaurus and the plant-eating nodosaur were discovered by paleontologists at Rabbit Valley.

Egg Mountain
Montana

The herd of duck-billed *Maiasauri* had crossed a wide plain to reach these forested hills. A small group of them watched as others worked busily beside a stream. The workers dug and mounded the moist dirt with their strong hind legs. Then they hollowed out the centers of the mounds with their noses and front legs. Soon, bowl-like piles of dirt three feet high and six feet wide were everywhere.

Every year, the maiasaurs came to this place to build these mounds. They were nests in which the mother dinosaurs would lay their eggs and raise their young. The eggs were arranged in circles around the inside of the nests. When one layer filled the bottom, the mother would lay a second layer on top. Each maiasaur scraped plants over the top of its eggs to help keep them warm.

Each nest held about twenty rounded eggs about the size of ostrich eggs— about ten inches long and five inches in diameter. Soon, the shells cracked and small heads popped out. The eggshells fell to the bottom of the nest and were trampled to bits by tiny dinosaur feet.

The newborn maiasaurs were about one foot long—much smaller than their gigantic mothers! And they were hungry! Their tiny squeaks told the adults they'd better get busy. To feed their young, the adults ate berries from nearby bushes and chewed them well. Then they spit out the berries at the edge of the nest for the babies to eat.

The baby maiasaurs grew quickly. Soon they were three feet long. Their nests became crowded, but they stayed where they were. They couldn't protect themselves from meat-eating dinosaurs.

Sometimes disasters killed baby maiasaurs. Maybe rain soaked the nesting ground for several days, and the stream overflowed its banks. Water lapped at the edges

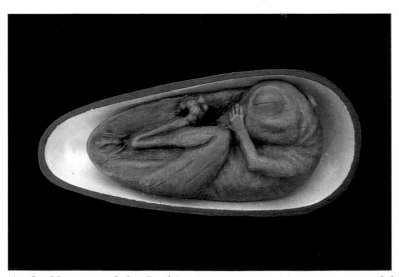

At the Museum of the Rockies in Bozeman, Montana, a model dinosaur egg holds its tiny cargo. PHOTO BY STEVE JACKSON.

of some of the nests. Unaware of the danger to their babies, the adults fled to higher ground. The little ones waited in their nests for their mothers to return. They were hungry and wet.

The babies were probably frightened by the water, but they may have been more afraid to leave the nest. So they stayed and they drowned. When the water receded, the nesting ground was a muddy mess, and there were dead maiasaurs everywhere. Some were still in the nests, while others had been washed out. The adults never returned that year. It was too late to lay more eggs.

Eventually, more floods filled the nests with mud and covered the bones of some of the baby maiasaurs. Eighty million years later, scientists dug up the fossilized bones and pieces of eggshell in the remote badlands of north-central Montana. They shared the story of *Maiasaura* with us all.

Paleontologists learned three important things about maiasaurs from the bones they found. Because so many nests were found in one place, scientists concluded that maiasaurs migrated to a special place to lay their eggs and raise their young. Modern birds that nest in colonies build their nests as far apart as their wingspans. If the maiasaurs did the same, they must have been twenty-three feet long. That was the average distance between nests.

The scientists also could see that the fossilized bones weren't developed on the ends. This meant that the babies were unable to support their own weight. They couldn't walk. The adults would have had to feed them in the nests. This was the first clue that some kinds of dinosaurs took care of their young.

Egg Mountain is near Choteau, Montana. You can reach it by driving ninety miles south of Glacier National Park on Highway 89, 125 miles north of Helena on Interstate 15 and Highway 287, or sixty miles west of Great Falls on Interstate 15 and Highway 89.

You can tour Egg Mountain at 2:30 p.m. daily between July 1 and August 20. The Museum of the Rockies in Bozeman, where some of the Egg Mountain finds are exhibited, sponsors a paleontology field school for adults and children. Participants get a chance to dig dinosaur bones with paleontologists at Egg Mountain for a week during the summers.

For more information contact:

> Museum of the Rockies
> Montana State University
> 600 West Kagy Boulevard
> Bozeman, Montana 59717
> (406) 994-2251 or 994-5257

Paleontologists working at Egg Mountain in Montana were the first to discover evidence that some dinosaur mothers took care of their young. By studying the eighty-million-year-old nests of some duck-billed maiasaurs, they learned that the young depended on their mothers to feed them.

Clayton Lake State Park
New Mexico

A chilling rain had been falling for days. A herd of large duckbills, or hadrosaurs, sought refuge from the cold in a dense forest not far from the sea. When the sun finally broke through one morning, the dinosaurs left the forest to search for fresh water to drink.

One hadrosaur wandered away from the rest and found a small pond at the edge of the trees. The water was inviting, but a muddy hillside stood between the dinosaur and a drink. How could the animal get to the water?

As the hadrosaur started down the muddy hill, its feet slipped and slid through the ooze. To steady itself, the huge animal braced its tail against the ground. The tail, which it usually held out stiffly behind it, dragged through the mud. It helped to balance the hadrosaur so that it was able to get to the pond.

Fossilized tracks tell the story of how dinosaurs moved about. This hadrosaur's tracks were preserved in sandstone and discovered 100 million years later at Clayton Lake State Park. They reveal one way that dinosaurs may have moved from place to place on slippery surfaces. Slip marks in the tracks and a groove that passes through the heel of several tracks have led paleontologists to believe that this particular hadrosaur braced itself with its tail.

The tracks of many kinds of dinosaurs have been found at Clayton Lake State Park. Most were made by heavy dinosaurs that may have walked on two feet. It's not always possible to identify a species of dinosaur by its tracks. But they can be put into general groups. At Clayton Lake State Park, three meat-eating dinosaur groups have been identified by their tracks: one small and birdlike, one heavy and large, and one that may have had webbed feet.

More than 500 tracks here indicate that many of these dinosaurs were milling around. Their tracks don't head in one specific direction. Some are in lines and can be identified as one individual dinosaur. Others are tracks on top of tracks. One set of tracks, called the "dinosaur shuffle," shows an animal definitely hesitating, stepping forward and back several times.

The best time to see dinosaur tracks at the park is in early morning or late afternoon, when the sun casts shadows in them. Educational facilities at the park include a pavilion overlooking the tracks and a boardwalk through the tracks that's marked with informative signs.

Clayton Lake State Park is 12.2 miles north of Clayton, New Mexico, from

State Road 370. It's open year-round. Access to the tracks is via a quarter-mile dirt and gravel trail. Admission to the park for the day is $3 or a New Mexico park permit.

For more information, contact:

Park Superintendent
Clayton Lake State Park
Seneca, New Mexico 88437
(505) 374-8808

Clayton Lake State Park features more than 500 tracks of many kinds of dinosaurs. Photo by Mike Blus.

A muddy hillside didn't stop this hadrosaur from quenching its thirst in a nearby pond. Using its tail to steady itself, it slid down through the ooze. The groove made by the tail can still be seen today, 100 million years later, at Clayton Lake State Park, New Mexico.

Dinosaur Valley State Park
Texas

Trees and low plants flourished in the moist climate. The sea had receded, exposing large stretches of mud and coral reefs. The reefs acted as dams. Shallow, saltwater lagoons formed behind them.

A group of sauropods—large, plant-eating dinosaurs—ambled across the mud toward a lagoon. They had followed this route many times. They swayed from side to side as they walked, trying not to bump into each other.

Today, more than 105 million years later, you can see the saucerlike footprints left by these lumbering dinosaurs at Dinosaur Valley State Park.

Parts of another trackway at the park were removed in 1940. They showed a set of sauropod tracks followed by the tracks of a large, meat-eating dinosaur. This record of an ancient hunt was reassembled beneath a brontosaur skeleton at the American Museum of Natural History in New York City. A cast of the tracks is on display at the visitor center at Dinosaur Valley State Park.

Generally, three kinds of dinosaur tracks have been discovered at the park. The most common ones look like the footprints of three-toed birds, but they're twelve to twenty-four inches long and nine to seventeen inches wide. They apparently belong to a smaller relative of the *Tyrannosaurus* known as *Acrocanthosaurus*.

The second most common tracks look like huge ovals pushed deep into the mud. Only sauropods are large enough to have left tracks three feet long and two feet wide.

The third kind of footprint may be that of a two-legged plant-eater related to the later duckbills. But these tracks also could be poorly imprinted tracks of the *Acrocanthosaurus*. They remain a mystery.

Tracks at the park have been used to figure out how fast these dinosaurs moved. By measuring the distance between tracks and comparing it to the length of the dinosaur's legs, scientists have determined that the meat-eaters traveled at five miles an hour, while the plant-eaters went 2.7 miles an hour.

Dinosaur Valley State Park is about fifty-eight miles southwest of Fort Worth, near the town of Glen Rose. From Glen Rose, travel four miles west on Farm Road 205 to Park Road 59. From there, it's one mile to park headquarters. Towering over the park are fiberglass models of a seventy-foot *Apatosaurus* and a forty-five-foot *Tyrannosaurus*. The visitor center is open daily between 8 a.m. and 5 p.m.

For more information, contact:

Dinosaur Valley State Park
Box 396
Glen Rose, Texas 76043
(817) 897-4588

Left. *A sauropod made these tracks in what is now Texas.* PHOTOS COURTESY OF DINOSAUR VALLEY STATE PARK.

Above. *The fiberglass model of a* Tyrannosaurus *welcomes visitors to Dinosaur Valley State Park.*

Saucerlike footprints at Dinosaur Valley State Park in Texas show that a herd of sauropods lumbered through the mud here more than 105 million years ago. Two other kinds of tracks indicate they shared the area with the meat-eating Acrocanthosaurus *and possibly a two-legged plant-eater related to the later duckbills.*

Dinosaur National Monument
Utah and Colorado

A river wandered across the wide, flat plain, fed by many small streams that ran only when it rained. The climate was usually dry. Tall trees and a variety of ferns grew along the banks of the river and streams.

Turtles and crocodiles lived in the river and sometimes sunned themselves on its broad sandbars. Many species of dinosaurs lived along the river. The plantlife attracted hungry plant-eaters, which in turn attracted meat-eaters.

This particular morning had been sunny and warm, but the afternoon sky was dark and thick with clouds. High in the hills, it was raining hard, and the small streams flowed. Plants and soil were washed downstream. Even the body of a dinosaur that had recently died floated toward the river. It finally got hung up on a sandbar, and there it stayed.

For many years, as dinosaurs died near the river, their bones washed downstream and lodged against the ever-growing pile of bones at the sandbar. Over time, the river vanished, and other rivers and seas took its place. They piled layers of sediment over the dinosaur bones. The sediments became rock and preserved the bones as fossils. Years later, scientists uncovered them at a site twenty miles east of Vernal, Utah. They pieced together this story from the arrangement of the bones.

Nearly twenty complete dinosaur skeletons and many incomplete ones have been found at the quarry at Dinosaur National Monument. Turtles, frogs, crocodiles, and clams also have become part of the story, since their bones and shells have been found in the same rocks as the dinosaur bones.

Fifteen species of animals have been discovered here, most of them dinosaurs. Several are sauropods, or reptile-footed plant-eaters. A few are theropods (beast-footed meat-eaters), and a couple others are ornithopods (bird-footed plant-eaters).

The dinosaur quarry where the first remains were discovered is now enclosed by a building. From a two-story gallery, you can see the face of the quarry, as well as the laboratory where paleontologists work on the fossils.

You can reach the quarry by driving north from Jensen, Utah, on Highway 149 and following the signs. There is a $5 admission fee per vehicle to enter Dinosaur National Monument.

Left. *Workers finish chipping the rock from around some of the almost twenty complete skeletons at the Dinosaur National Monument quarry.* PHOTOS BY NATIONAL PARK SERVICE.

Above. *You can see the face of the dinosaur quarry from a two-story gallery.*

For more information, contact the Quarry Visitor Center at:

> Dinosaur National Monument
> Box 128
> Jensen, Utah 84035
> (801) 789-2115

Or you may contact park headquarters at:

> Dinosaur National Monument
> Box 210
> Dinosaur, Colorado 81610
> (303) 374-2216

The quarry at Dinosaur National Monument tells the story of the many forms of life that lived along this ancient river in what is now Utah and Colorado. The ferns growing along the banks attracted plant-eaters, which in turn attracted meat-eaters. Fifteen species of animals have been discovered here, most of them dinosaurs.

Cleveland-Lloyd Dinosaur Quarry
Utah

No streams flowed into the quiet valley. The lush vegetation depended instead upon rainwater for moisture. There was one shallow watering hole, surrounded by evergreen trees and shrubs.

A small group of allosaurs headed for the watering hole, thirsty after crossing the valley and nearby plains. Some of the young dinosaurs weighed fewer than 100 pounds and couldn't travel as fast as the four-ton adults. The group stopped often so the young ones could catch up. The meat-eaters didn't travel in large packs because there wasn't enough prey to feed more than a small group.

As they neared the water, the allosaurs could see a dead dinosaur lying in it. The leaders of the group began to feed on the carcass. But the bottom of the watering hole was soft mud, and the allosaurs couldn't pull their feet out of the ooze as they gathered around their meal. They struggled to get free, but finally, like the dinosaur they'd found in the water, they died.

Other hungry allosaurs came along later. They, too, thought they'd found an easy meal. But they, too, became stuck in the mud when they approached the dead bodies already trapped there. Each dead dinosaur attracted another hungry dinosaur until more than forty allosaurs had piled on top of each other in the muck.

The sharp teeth of the meat-eating Allosaurus *are still frightening even 147 million years later.* PHOTO COURTESY OF CLEVELAND-LLOYD DINOSAUR QUARRY.

Eventually, the bones scattered and the watering hole dried up. Volcanoes covered the area in ash, and rivers and seas deposited thick layers of sand and mud. The bones became fossilized. For about 147 million years, the bones of the dinosaurs lay hidden until wind and water eroded the rock away and the petrified bones became visible once again.

This discovery at Cleveland-Lloyd Dinosaur Quarry has yielded the most complete collection ever found of *Allosauri* in various stages of development. As a result, scientists have been able to put together many skeletons to see how these large dinosaurs grew.

The *Allosaurus* is the state fossil of Utah. A twenty-two-foot skeleton mounted in the visitor center at the quarry is of a juvenile *Allosaurus* that would have been about thirteen years old in human years. As young as it was, it was a fierce predator.

The bones of at least ten different kinds of dinosaurs have been found where the watering hole once was. About two-thirds of them were *Allosaurus* bones. Paleontologists also have found the remains of the plant-eating *Stegosaurus, Camarasaurus*, and *Camptosaurus.*

Another interesting discovery made at Cleveland-Lloyd was a dinosaur egg. It contains an unborn dinosaur, and scientists believe the egg was in the mother's womb when she died.

Cleveland-Lloyd Dinosaur Quarry became a National Natural Landmark in 1966. As a result, it receives special protection under federal law. The visitor center is operated by the Bureau of Land Management. It has displays providing information about discoveries made here and other more general displays explaining dinosaurs and how they lived.

The quarry has been covered with steel buildings to protect it. Many bones can be seen from a deck suspended above this area. Excavations continue.

The quarry is open weekends from Easter weekend through Memorial weekend and then daily through the summer until Labor Day. Hours are 10 a.m. to 5 p.m. The quarry is located about thirty miles south of Price, Utah. The last twelve miles are via well-kept dirt roads.

For more information, write or call:

> Cleveland-Lloyd Dinosaur Quarry
> c/o Bureau of Land Management
> 900 North 700 East
> Price, Utah 84501
> (801) 637-4584

What appeared to be an easy meal turned into a death trap for this four-ton Allosaurus. Caught in the ooze as it tried to feed on a dead dinosaur, it died, and its bones were preserved as fossils. You can see them today at Cleveland-Lloyd Dinosaur Quarry in Utah.

Dinosaur Museums of the West

ALBERTA, CANADA

Royal Tyrrell Museum of Palaeontology, Box 7500, Drumheller, Alberta, Canada T0J 0Y0, (403) 823-7707

Opened in 1985, this is one of the largest paleontological museums in the world. Exhibits trace 4.5 billion years of earth's history. One gallery contains thirty-five complete dinosaur skeletons, the largest number assembled under one roof anywhere in the world. Also featured are murals, slide shows, video mini-theaters, computer stations, hands-on scientific experiments, and a plant "palaeoconservatory."

ARIZONA

Museum of Northern Arizona, Route 4, Box 720, Flagstaff, Arizona 86001, (602) 774-5211

This museum features the skeletons of two dinosaurs found only in Arizona: a double-crested meat-eater called *Dilophosaurus* and one of the first armored dinosaurs, *Scutellosaurus*. Also featured is the skeleton of *Coelophysis*, one of the oldest known dinosaurs of North America.

CALIFORNIA

California Academy of Sciences, Golden Gate Park, San Francisco, California 94118, (415) 750-7145 for recorded information

The academy opened its "Life Through Time" exhibit in 1990, with more than sixty displays demonstrating how life has evolved. Dioramas show early life under the sea, a forest scene with a robotic eight-foot millipede and two-foot scorpion, and a Montana dig site where academy scientists discovered the remains of a *Triceratops*. Other exhibits discuss dinosaur mothering, the similarities between dinosaurs and birds, and the theories about why dinosaurs became extinct. Living animals help to demonstrate how some lifeforms have evolved very little over time. An interactive computer video called "LifeMap" allows you to trace the evolution of any animal, living or extinct. A hologram of a *Tyrannosaurus* skull is one of the most popular attractions.

Museum of Paleontology, 3 Earth Sciences Building, University of California, Berkeley, California 94720, (510) 642-1821

This museum features the skeletons of several dinosaurs found in the West, including two duckbills. One has the characteristic "beak" that gave the creature its name. The other has an unusual crest on the top of its head. The cast of a *Tyrannosaurus* skull is also on display. Each March, the museum holds an open house with films, activities, and the chance to talk to paleontologists. A Young People's Lecture Series is conducted in the spring and occasionally in the fall.

Natural History Museum of Los Angeles County, 900 Exposition Boulevard, Los Angeles, California 90007, (213) 744-DINO for recorded information, (213) 744-3414 for other information

The huge *Tyrannosaurus* skull on exhibit here has been the model for casts on display in many museums around the world. The skeletons of a plant-eating *Camptosaurus* and a fierce *Allosaurus* are posed as if locked in battle. Also on display are the skull of a *Triceratops*, as well as the full skeleton of a *Stegosaurus* and a three-toed footprint of an unknown dinosaur.

COLORADO

Denver Museum of Natural History, 2001 Colorado Boulevard, Denver, Colorado 80205, (303) 322-7009, (303) 370-8257 for the hearing impaired

The life-sized cast of a twenty-foot-tall *Tyrannosaurus* greets visitors as they enter, and a cast of the ferocious meat-eater's skull lurks within. Also featured are the skeletons of a *Stegosaurus*, Colorado's official state fossil, and a *Diplodocus*, one of the longest of all dinosaurs and the central focus of the fossil area. You may watch as dinosaur fossils are prepared for exhibit at the Schlessman Family Earth Sciences Laboratory.

Dinosaur Valley, 362 Main Street, Grand Junction, Colorado 81501, (303) 241-9210

Dinosaur Valley is the natural history division of the Museum of Western Colorado. The exhibit includes several half-sized dinosaur replicas. Also on display is an *Allosaurus* skeleton, as well as other fossils and tracks. You may watch fossil preparation at an on-site laboratory.

University of Colorado Museum, Hendersen Building, 15th and Broadway, Boulder, Colorado 80309, (303) 492-6165 weekdays, (303) 492-6892 weekends

Dinosaur fossils are accompanied by labels that explain each animal's size, habitat, diet, speed, and type of birth. Featured are a *Triceratops* skull and the three-foot-wide footprint of a duckbill. Life-sized wall murals of dinosaurs in action show how they moved and attacked prey. A video explains fossil-finding expeditions led by scientists from the university.

MONTANA

Museum of the Rockies, Montana State University, 600 West Kagy Boulevard, Bozeman, Montana 59717, (406) 994-2251

An animated model of a *Triceratops* mother with her young roars and charges at you as you enter the paleontology display. Also featured are a *Triceratops* skull and models of the *Maiasaura peeblesorum*, a duckbill discovered with its nest in Montana. It has been named the official state fossil. At the Bowman Fossil Bank, you may watch volunteers prepare fossil specimens for paleontological research. A hands-on Discovery Room and a planetarium show allow for further discoveries. The museum also sponsors summer paleontological field schools for adults and children.

NEW MEXICO

New Mexico Museum of Natural History, 1801 Mountain Road NW, Albuquerque, New Mexico 87104, (505) 841-8836

Two life-sized bronze dinosaur sculptures welcome you to the museum grounds. One is *Pentaceratops*, a five-horned dinosaur found only in New Mexico. The other is the fearsome killer *Albertosaurus*. Inside, you can ride the "Evolator," an elevator-like "time machine" that uses a computer and video to teach you about New Mexico's geologic history and the creatures that roamed here during the Cretaceous Period, seventy-five million years ago. There are also life-sized casts of *Allosaurus, Camarasaurus,* and *Stegosaurus,* as well as a life-sized model of the official state fossil, *Coelophysis*. One special exhibit includes four vertebrae of a *Seismosaurus*, which may have been the longest animal ever to have lived. The rest of the dinosaur is still being excavated in northwestern New Mexico.

SASKATCHEWAN, CANADA

Saskatchewan Musuem of Natural History, Wascana Park, Regina, Saskatchewan, Canada S4P 3V7, (306) 787-2815

In the Earth Sciences Gallery, a dinosaur diorama includes models of *Tyrannosaurus, Troodon, Ankylosaurus, Edmontosaurus,* and *Triceratops*. There is also a half-sized animated model of a *Tyrannosaurus*. A huge *Triceratops* skull revolves on a turntable, and a bird-hipped *Thescelosaurus* is mounted on the wall. In the "Paleo-Pit," you can examine fossilized plants and animals up close, and there is space to make models, see videos, put together puzzles, and make rubbings of fossils. You may also watch fossil preparation at an on-site laboratory.

UTAH

Utah Field House of Natural History State Park, 235 East Main Street, Vernal, Utah 84078-2605, (801) 789-3799

The main features of the park are the museum and Dinosaur Gardens. The museum displays the fossilized remains of *Stegosaurus* and *Diplodocus*, as well as dinosaur tracks. The outdoor garden is inhabited by fifteen full-sized replicas of prehistoric animals exhibited in surroundings resembling their homes of millions of years ago. From Thanksgiving to New Year's Day, more than 75,000 lights illuminate the garden.

Utah Museum of Natural History, University of Utah, Salt Lake City, Utah 84112, (801) 581-4303

Four full skeletons of dinosaurs from the Cleveland-Lloyd Quarry are on display. Posed in lifelike positions are two *Allosauri*, a *Stegosaurus*, and a *Camptosaurus*. There is also a reconstructed dinosaur nest with replica eggs like those found at the quarry. The fossilized bones of an *Apatosaurus'* huge hind leg are mounted against a wall mural depicting the animal as it may have looked in life. An audio tape explains the dinosaurs that once lived in Utah. The museum also sponsors field trips, classes, and workshops.

Brigham Young University Earth Science Museum, 1683 North Canyon Road, Provo, Utah 84602, (801) 378-3680

The museum's collection of dinosaur fossils from the Jurassic period is among the best in the world. It includes remains of the largest dinosaurs yet discovered, the *Ultrasaurus* and the *Supersaurus*. There are also displays of *Tyrannosaurus* and *Triceratops*, as well as some displays on loan from the Smithsonian Institution. In one display, a CAT scan of a dinosaur egg reveals the fossilized embryo inside. At a special "touch table," you may study fossils up close.

College of Eastern Utah Prehistoric Museum, 451 East 400 North, Price, Utah 84501, (801) 637-5060

In the Hall of Dinosaurs, a huge sandbox contains the upright skeletons of *Allosaurus* and *Camptosaurus*. The skeletons of *Stegosaurus* and *Camarasaurus* lie in the sand in the same positions in which they were discovered. Also on display are the remains of the crested *Prosaurolophus*, the long-frilled *Chasmosaurus*, the armored *Nodosaurus*, and some new, unnamed dinosaurs. The museum holds one of the largest collections of dinosaur tracks in the country. You may watch fossil preparation in an on-site laboratory.

WYOMING

The Geological Museum, University of Wyoming, Laramie, Wyoming 82071-3006, (307) 766-4218

A copper statue of a *Tyrannosaurus* stands outside the museum. Inside, the complete skeleton of an *Apatosaurus* stretches from one end of the building to the other. You can also see the cast of a juvenile *Maiasaura* and the fossilized skulls of the long-frilled *Anchicerotops* and duckbill *Anatosaurus*. At one display, you can literally get a feel for dinosaur skin.